Contents

Preface: 6
Part I: The Foundations of Artificial Thought 8
  Chapter 1: The Seeds of Artificial Thought: From Myth to Logic 8
    Defining Artificial Intelligence: A Multifaceted Concept 8
    Mythological Precursors: Imagining Artificial Life 9
    Philosophical Foundations: The Dawn of Logical Thought 10
    Conceptual Questions: Seeds of Scientific Inquiry 10
  Chapter 2: The Mechanical Dawn of Computation: Building the First Thinking Machines (in Principle) 11
    Early Mechanical Calculating Devices: Automating Arithmetic 11
    Charles Babbage and the Engines: A Vision of Programmable Computation 12
    Ada Lovelace: Recognizing the Potential of General-Purpose Computation 13
    Limitations and Legacy: Paving the Way for Electronic Computation 13
Part II: The Birth and Evolution of AI 15
  Chapter 3: The Rise of the Electronic Age: From Valves to the Turing Machine 15
    The Dawn of Electronic Computation: Wartime Necessity and Innovation 15
    The Turing Machine: A Theoretical Foundation for Computation 16
    The Turing Test: A Benchmark for Machine Intelligence .. 17

From Theory to Practice: The Convergence of Ideas 17

Chapter 4: The Birth of AI as a Field: The Dartmouth Workshop and Early Promise 17

The Dartmouth Workshop: A Meeting of Interdisciplinary Minds 18

Early AI Programs: Demonstrating the Potential 18

The Rise of Symbolic AI: Focusing on Logic and Rules ...19

Early Optimism and the Challenges Ahead 19

Chapter 5: The Golden Age of AI: Expert Systems and the Pursuit of Intelligent Machines (1960s-Early 1970s)............20

Expert Systems: Capturing Human Expertise 20

Natural Language Processing: Communicating with Machines 21

Robotics and Early Machine Learning 22

The Limits of Early AI and the Seeds of Disillusionment ..22

Chapter 6: The AI Winter: A Period of Disillusionment and Reassessment (Late 1970s-Mid 1980s)...............................23

The Lighthill Report: A Critical Assessment......................23

The "Perceptrons" Critique: A Setback for Neural Networks 24

The Limitations of Symbolic AI: Knowledge Representation and Common Sense 25

A Period of Reassessment and New Directions 25

Chapter 7: The Connectionist Revolution: A Resurgence of Neural Networks (Mid-1980s-Early 1990s) 26

The Re-emergence of Neural Networks: Overcoming Past Limitations..26

- Key Figures and Research: Laying the Foundation for Deep Learning 27
- Early Applications and Renewed Interest 28
- From Connectionism to Deep Learning: The Next Step ... 28

Chapter 8: The Rise of Machine Learning: From Rules to Data (Late 1980s-2000s) 29
- The Shift to Data-Driven Approaches: Learning from Experience 29
- Key Paradigms of Machine Learning: Supervised, Unsupervised, and Reinforcement Learning 29
- Key Algorithms and Techniques: Expanding the Toolkit .. 31
- Applications and Impact: Bringing Machine Learning to the Real World 31
- Setting the Stage for Deep Learning: The Need for More Data and Computation 32

Chapter 9: The Big Data Revolution: Fueling the AI Boom (2000s-2010s) 32
- The Explosion of Data: Volume, Velocity, and Variety 33
- Advancements in Computing Infrastructure: Handling Massive Datasets 34
- The Impact on AI: Fueling Deep Learning and Other Applications 35
- Data as the New Currency: The Rise of Data-Driven Companies 35
- Ethical Considerations: Privacy, Bias, and Accountability 36

Chapter 10: The Deep Learning Breakthrough: A New Era of AI (2010s-Present) 36
- The Power of Deep Neural Networks: Learning Hierarchical Representations 37

- Key Architectural Innovations: CNNs and RNNs 37
- The ImageNet Moment: A Paradigm Shift in Image Recognition 38
- Natural Language Processing Breakthroughs: From Word Embeddings to Transformers 38
- Key Applications and Impact: Transforming Industries 39
- The Ongoing Evolution of Deep Learning: New Architectures and Techniques 40

Part III: The Future and Legacy of AI 41

Chapter 11: AI in Action: Transforming Industries and Everyday Life (2010s-Present) 41

- Healthcare: Revolutionizing Diagnosis, Treatment, and Drug Discovery 41
- Transportation: The Rise of Autonomous Vehicles 42
- Finance and Fintech: Automating Processes and Detecting Fraud 42
- Retail and E-commerce: Personalizing the Customer Experience 43
- Entertainment and Media: Creating and Distributing Content 44
- Everyday AI: Virtual Assistants and Smart Devices 44
- The Pervasiveness of AI: A Transforming Force 45

Chapter 12: The Challenges and Opportunities of AI: Ethical, Societal, and Economic Implications 45

- Ethical Considerations: Bias, Fairness, Accountability, and Transparency 45
- Societal Impacts: Job Displacement, Inequality, and Surveillance 47

Economic Implications: Productivity, Innovation, and the Future of Work 47

Opportunities: Augmenting Human Capabilities and Solving Global Challenges 48

The Need for Responsible AI Development and Deployment 48

Chapter 13: The Future of Human-AI Collaboration: Augmented Intelligence and the Quest for AGI 49

Augmented Intelligence: Enhancing Human Capabilities . 49

The Quest for Artificial General Intelligence (AGI): Towards Human-Level AI 50

The Future of Human-AI Interaction: A Symbiotic Relationship and Philosophical Implications 51

Chapter 14: The Legacy of AI: A Continuing Quest to Understand Intelligence 52

A Mirror to Ourselves: Understanding Human Cognition .. 53

A Catalyst for Technological Innovation: Transforming Industries and Society 53

A Continuing Dialogue: Ethical and Societal Implications 54

The Unfinished Story: A Journey of Exploration and Discovery and the Current State of the Field 54

Bibliography: Entirely accessed through Gemni & Claude 56

I. Foundational Texts and Historical Documents: 56

II. Books on the History of AI: 56

III. Works on Specific AI Subfields: 57

IV. Articles and Reports: 57

V. Online Resources: 57

VI. Books on Related Topics: 57

Glossary: 59
    A 59
    B 59
    C 60
    D 60
    E 61
    G 61
    H 61
    I 61
    K 61
    L 62
    M 62
    N 62
    P 62
    R 63
    S 63
    T 63
Endnote: Methodology & Purpose 64

Preface:

From the smartphones in our pockets to the algorithms shaping our online world, artificial intelligence is no longer a futuristic fantasy—it's a present reality. But the seeds of this revolution were sown long ago, in the myths, philosophies, and early scientific explorations of centuries past. *Mind Machines* tells that story, exploring the key moments, the brilliant minds, and the unexpected twists and turns that have shaped AI.

We begin by exploring the ancient roots of this quest, tracing the echoes of artificial beings in mythology and the first philosophical inquiries into the nature of mind. We then witness the dawn of computation, from ingenious mechanical calculators to the conceptual breakthroughs that foreshadowed the digital age. We then explore the development of electronic computers and the emergence of AI as a distinct scientific discipline, marked by the pivotal Dartmouth Workshop in 1956.

We explore the periods of both exuberant optimism and deep disillusionment that have characterized the field's history, from the early promise of expert systems to the setbacks of the "AI winters." We examine the resurgence of neural networks and the rise of machine learning, culminating in the deep learning revolution that has transformed AI in recent years.

Throughout this journey, we delve into the crucial ethical and societal questions that arise as AI becomes increasingly integrated into our lives. We consider the potential for bias in algorithms, the impact of automation on the job market, and the broader implications of creating increasingly intelligent machines—as well as the immense potential for AI to help us tackle global challenges like climate change and disease.

Mind Machines is written for a broad audience, using clear and accessible language to demystify complex concepts. Whether you're a student eager to learn about the history of technology, a tech enthusiast fascinated by the latest advancements in AI, or simply curious about the future of our increasingly interconnected world, *Mind Machines* will provide you with a clear and engaging overview of the fascinating history and the profound implications of artificial intelligence. Understanding this history is not merely an academic exercise; it is essential for navigating the complex ethical, societal, and economic challenges—and the extraordinary opportunities—that AI presents to our world today.

Part I: The Foundations of Artificial Thought

Chapter 1: The Seeds of Artificial Thought: From Myth to Logic

The story of artificial intelligence is not a tale of overnight invention but a long and winding narrative woven from threads of mythology, philosophy, mathematics, and ultimately, computation. Before the advent of computers and algorithms, the dream of creating artificial beings capable of thought and action existed in the human imagination for millennia. This chapter explores the earliest conceptual foundations of AI, tracing the development of ideas that would eventually give rise to a new scientific discipline. This chapter will also briefly touch upon the debate of whether true AI requires consciousness or simply the appearance of intelligent behavior, which will be explored in more depth later in this book.

Defining Artificial Intelligence: A Multifaceted Concept

Artificial Intelligence (AI) is a complex and multifaceted concept, encompassing a range of approaches and goals. At its core, AI seeks to create systems capable of performing tasks that typically require human intelligence. These tasks include:

- **Learning from experience:** Acquiring knowledge and improving performance over time through interaction with data and the environment.

- **Reasoning and problem-solving:** Drawing inferences, making deductions, and finding solutions to complex problems.

- **Perception and interpretation:** Processing and understanding sensory information from the environment, such as images, sounds, and text.

- **Natural language processing:** Understanding and generating human language, enabling communication between humans and machines.

- **Planning and decision-making:** Setting goals, developing strategies, and making choices to achieve desired outcomes.

It's important to note that there is no single, universally accepted definition of AI. The field is constantly evolving, and the definition of AI often depends on the specific context and application. A key debate within the field revolves around the nature of "true" AI. Does a system need to possess consciousness or sentience to be considered truly intelligent, or is the mere appearance of intelligent behavior sufficient? This distinction is crucial and will be explored further in later chapters. However, the core idea of creating machines that can perform tasks requiring human intelligence remains central to the field.

Mythological Precursors: Imagining Artificial Life

The desire to create artificial beings is an ancient one, predating even the earliest forms of scientific inquiry. Myths and legends from various cultures are replete with stories of artificial entities imbued with life, intelligence, and purpose. These narratives, while fantastical, reveal a deep-seated human fascination with the possibility of creating artificial intelligence.

The Greek myths provide several compelling examples. Hephaestus, the god of fire and craftsmanship, was said to have created mechanical servants of gold, capable of performing various tasks. The myth of Talos, a giant automaton made of bronze, tasked with guarding the island of Crete, explores themes of artificial sentinels and the potential dangers of artificial power.

Beyond Greek mythology, other cultures also explored similar themes. In ancient Chinese legends, stories of ingenious automatons crafted by skilled artisans can be found, showcasing a similar fascination with creating artificial beings. Similarly, some aspects of ancient Indian philosophy touched upon concepts related to mind and consciousness, which, while not directly about creating artificial minds, explored related philosophical territory.

In Jewish folklore, the Golem, a creature made of clay and brought to life through Kabbalistic rituals, represents a powerful metaphor for artificial creation and the ethical dilemmas that can arise from it. These stories, while not scientific in nature, demonstrate a long-standing human interest in the possibility of creating artificial life and intelligence. They also raise fundamental questions about the nature of creation, control, and the potential consequences of such endeavors.

Philosophical Foundations: The Dawn of Logical Thought

The philosophical foundations of AI can be traced back to the ancient Greek philosophers, who sought to systematize human thought and understand the nature of reason. Aristotle's work on logic, particularly his development of syllogistic reasoning, provided one of the first formal systems for representing and manipulating knowledge. Syllogisms, with their structured premises and logical conclusions, offered a model for deductive reasoning that would later influence the development of AI algorithms.

Centuries later, in the 17th century, Gottfried Wilhelm Leibniz envisioned a *characteristica universalis*, a universal language of reasoning based on symbolic notation. He believed that all rational thought could be expressed and manipulated mathematically within this system, allowing for the mechanization of reasoning. Leibniz's dream foreshadowed the development of formal logic, computer science, and the symbolic manipulation at the heart of early AI systems. His concept of a "calculus ratiocinator," a system for mechanically deriving conclusions from premises, was a direct precursor to automated reasoning systems.

Conceptual Questions: Seeds of Scientific Inquiry

These early explorations, while primarily philosophical and mythological, laid the conceptual groundwork for the scientific pursuit of AI. They raised fundamental questions that continue to drive AI research today:

- **Can thought be formalized?** Can the processes of reasoning, learning, and perception be reduced to a set of rules or algorithms?

- **Is the mind a machine?** Can mental processes be understood as computations performed by a physical system?

- **What is the nature of consciousness?** Can machines be conscious, and if so, how would we know?

- **What are the ethical implications of creating intelligent machines?** What are the potential benefits and risks of artificial intelligence?

By the early 20th century, these philosophical musings began to transition from abstract speculation into a nascent scientific discipline. The groundwork laid by thinkers like Aristotle and Leibniz provided the intellectual scaffolding for the mathematicians, logicians, and computer scientists who would eventually bring artificial intelligence into existence.

Chapter 2: The Mechanical Dawn of Computation: Building the First Thinking Machines (in Principle)

The transition from philosophical musings about intelligence to the creation of actual calculating machines marked a crucial step on the path to artificial intelligence. While these early devices were primarily designed for mathematical computation, they introduced fundamental concepts that would later become cornerstones of modern computing and AI. This chapter explores the key developments in mechanical computation, highlighting the ingenuity of early inventors, the limitations they faced due to the available manufacturing techniques, and the crucial conceptual foundations they laid.

Early Mechanical Calculating Devices: Automating Arithmetic

The first attempts to mechanize computation focused on automating basic arithmetic operations. In 1623, Wilhelm Schickard, a German professor, designed the "Calculating Clock," a machine capable of performing addition, subtraction, multiplication, and division. Although Schickard's machine was a significant invention, it remained relatively unknown for centuries due to its incomplete documentation and the destruction of the prototype during the Thirty Years' War.

A more widely recognized early calculating machine is the Pascaline, invented by Blaise Pascal in 1642. Pascal, a French mathematician and philosopher, developed the Pascaline to assist his father, a tax collector, with his calculations. The Pascaline used a series of interconnected gears to perform addition and subtraction. While limited in its functionality, the Pascaline demonstrated the feasibility of mechanizing arithmetic operations and inspired further innovations in mechanical computation.

Gottfried Wilhelm Leibniz, whom we encountered in the previous chapter for his philosophical contributions, also made significant contributions to mechanical computation. In the 1670s, Leibniz designed the "Stepped Reckoner," a more advanced calculating machine that could perform multiplication and division through repeated addition and subtraction. The Stepped Reckoner introduced the concept of a stepped drum, a cylindrical component with teeth of increasing length, which simplified the process of multiplication.

Charles Babbage and the Engines: A Vision of Programmable Computation

The most significant advancements in mechanical computation came in the 19th century with the work of Charles Babbage, an English mathematician and inventor. Babbage conceived two remarkable machines: the Difference Engine and the Analytical Engine.

The Difference Engine, conceived in the 1820s, was designed to automate the calculation of polynomial functions, which were used to create mathematical tables for navigation and other scientific purposes. Babbage secured funding from the British government to build the Difference Engine, but the project was ultimately abandoned due to technological limitations, escalating costs, and the sheer complexity of manufacturing the precise components required.

However, Babbage's most ambitious project was the Analytical Engine, designed in the 1830s. The Analytical Engine was a general-purpose computing machine, far more advanced than any previous calculating device. It incorporated several key features that are fundamental to modern computers:

- **Programmable Instructions:** The Engine was designed to be programmed using punched cards, similar to those used in Jacquard looms for weaving patterns. This allowed users to input different sequences of instructions to perform different calculations. This was a revolutionary concept, as it meant that the machine could be adapted to perform a wide range of tasks, not just pre-defined calculations.
- **Memory Unit ("Store"):** The Engine had a "store," a memory unit capable of storing numbers and intermediate results. This allowed the

machine to perform complex calculations that required storing and retrieving data.

- **Central Processing Unit ("Mill"):** The "mill" was the Engine's equivalent of a central processing unit, where the actual arithmetic operations were performed on the data stored in the "store."

- **Conditional Control (Branching):** The Engine was designed to perform conditional jumps, allowing it to execute different instructions based on the results of previous calculations. This is a crucial element of modern programming, enabling complex decision-making processes.

Ada Lovelace: Recognizing the Potential of General-Purpose Computation

Ada Lovelace, the daughter of Lord Byron, was a mathematician and writer who played a crucial role in understanding the potential of the Analytical Engine. She translated an article about Babbage's Analytical Engine by Italian engineer Luigi Menabrea and added her own extensive notes. In these notes, Lovelace went beyond simply describing the machine's calculating abilities. She recognized that the Analytical Engine could manipulate symbols according to rules, suggesting that it could potentially compose music, create graphics, or perform other tasks beyond numerical computation.

Lovelace's most significant contribution was her understanding that the Analytical Engine was not just a calculator but a general-purpose computing device. She articulated the concept of an algorithm—a sequence of instructions that could be executed by a machine—and even wrote what is considered the first algorithm intended to be carried out by a machine, for calculating Bernoulli numbers. This insight was decades ahead of its time and laid the groundwork for the development of computer programming.

Limitations and Legacy: Paving the Way for Electronic Computation

Despite their ingenuity, the mechanical computing devices of this era faced significant limitations. They were complex, bulky, expensive to build, and prone to mechanical errors. The precision required for the intricate gears, levers, and other mechanical components of Babbage's engines was beyond the capabilities of 19th-century engineering. While a small part of the Analytical Engine's "mill" was constructed by Babbage's son Henry and successfully demonstrated, the full Analytical Engine was never completed during Charles Babbage's lifetime.

However, the mechanical era was crucial in establishing the fundamental concepts of computation. Babbage's ideas of programmable instructions, memory, processing, and conditional control became cornerstones of modern computer architecture. Lovelace's vision of general-purpose computation and her understanding of algorithms foreshadowed the very essence of computer programming and the potential for artificial intelligence. These conceptual breakthroughs paved the way for the electronic revolution that would follow, enabling the creation of machines that could not only calculate but also process information and, eventually, exhibit forms of artificial intelligence.

Part II: The Birth and Evolution of AI

Chapter 3: The Rise of the Electronic Age: From Valves to the Turing Machine

The mechanical calculators of the previous era, while groundbreaking in concept, were ultimately limited by the technology of their time. The 20th century brought forth a technological revolution—electronics—that would not only transform computation but also provide the necessary foundation for the realization of artificial intelligence. This chapter explores the key developments in electronic computing that paved the way for the birth of AI as a scientific field, focusing on the crucial role of vacuum tubes (or valves, as they were known in Britain) and the profound theoretical contributions of Alan Turing.

The Dawn of Electronic Computation: Wartime Necessity and Innovation

The pressures of World War II significantly accelerated the development of electronic computing. The need for rapid calculations in ballistics, cryptography, and other military applications spurred substantial investment and innovation. In the United States, the ENIAC (Electronic Numerical Integrator and Computer), unveiled in 1946, became a symbol of this new era.

The ENIAC was a colossal machine, weighing nearly 30 tons and occupying a large room. It used vacuum tubes (electronic devices that control the flow of electric current) to perform calculations. Unlike mechanical calculators, which relied on physical gears and levers, the ENIAC's electronic components allowed for significantly faster computation. It could perform calculations in minutes that would have taken human mathematicians days or even weeks. However, programming the ENIAC was a laborious process involving physically rewiring the machine.

Parallel developments were taking place in Britain at Bletchley Park, a top-secret codebreaking facility. A team led by Tommy Flowers developed the Colossus computers. These machines were designed to break German encryption codes generated by the Lorenz cipher machine. The Colossus, while its existence was kept secret for many years after the war, was a crucial milestone in electronic computing. It demonstrated the power of electronic machines for complex information processing and played a vital role in the Allied war effort. Unlike the ENIAC, which required rewiring for each new program, the Colossus used electronic switching, making it programmable via patch cables and switches. It is also important to note that the Colossus used electronic *valves* (the British term for vacuum tubes). The Colossus was designed for a specific purpose – codebreaking – and thus was not considered a general-purpose computer like the ENIAC.

The Turing Machine: A Theoretical Foundation for Computation

While the ENIAC and Colossus represented significant practical advancements, the most profound theoretical work of this era came from the brilliant mathematician Alan Turing. In his 1936 paper "On Computable Numbers, with an Application to the Entscheidungsproblem," Turing introduced the concept of the Turing Machine.

The Turing Machine is not a physical machine but a theoretical model of computation. It consists of an infinitely long tape divided into cells, a read/write head that can move along the tape, and a finite set of rules that dictate the head's actions based on the symbol it reads in the current cell. Despite its simplicity, the Turing Machine is incredibly powerful. Turing demonstrated that any computation that can be performed by an algorithm can also be performed by a Turing Machine.

This concept, known as the Church-Turing thesis (named also after Alonzo Church who independently developed a similar concept called Lambda calculus), has profound implications for computer science and AI. It establishes that any computable problem can be solved by a mechanical procedure, whether implemented by a human, a mechanical device, or an electronic computer. This provided a theoretical foundation for the idea that machines could perform tasks that require intelligence.

Turing's work also directly influenced the development of the first electronic computers built after the war. For example, the Manchester Small-Scale Experimental Machine (SSEM), also known as "Baby," built in 1948, was directly inspired by Turing's theoretical work on computation.

The Turing Test: A Benchmark for Machine Intelligence

Turing's contributions extended beyond theoretical computation. In his 1950 paper "Computing Machinery and Intelligence," he proposed the Turing Test, a thought experiment designed to address the question "Can machines think?"

The Turing Test involves a human evaluator engaging in natural language conversations with both a human and a machine, without knowing which is which. If the evaluator cannot reliably distinguish the machine from the human based on their responses, the machine is said to have passed the Turing Test.

The Turing Test has become a significant benchmark in the field of AI, sparking debate and research into natural language processing, knowledge representation, and other areas crucial for creating truly intelligent machines. While no machine has definitively passed the Turing Test in its most stringent form, it continues to be a valuable tool for evaluating progress in AI.

From Theory to Practice: The Convergence of Ideas

The development of electronic computers like the ENIAC and Colossus, combined with Turing's theoretical work on computation and machine intelligence, created a fertile ground for the emergence of AI as a scientific discipline. The ability to build machines that could perform complex calculations at unprecedented speeds, coupled with the theoretical framework for understanding computation and intelligence, set the stage for the pioneers who would gather at Dartmouth in 1956 and formally launch the field of artificial intelligence.

Chapter 4: The Birth of AI as a Field: The Dartmouth Workshop and Early Promise

The technological advancements of the electronic age, combined with decades of philosophical and theoretical groundwork, culminated in a pivotal moment in the summer of 1956: the Dartmouth Summer Research Project on Artificial Intelligence. This workshop, held at Dartmouth College in Hanover, New Hampshire, is widely considered the official birth of artificial intelligence as a distinct scientific field.

The Dartmouth Workshop: A Meeting of Interdisciplinary Minds

The workshop was the brainchild of John McCarthy, a then-young mathematician at Dartmouth College. He envisioned a gathering of brilliant minds to explore the possibility of creating machines that could think. Securing funding from the Rockefeller Foundation, McCarthy brought together a diverse group of researchers, including Marvin Minsky (a mathematician and cognitive scientist from MIT), Nathaniel Rochester (an information theorist from IBM), and Claude Shannon (a mathematician and electrical engineer from Bell Labs), among others. The attendees represented a variety of disciplines, including mathematics, psychology, computer science, and linguistics, highlighting the interdisciplinary nature of the nascent field of AI.

The proposal for the workshop boldly stated: "We propose that a 2 month, 10 man study of artificial intelligence be carried out during the summer of 1956 at Dartmouth College in Hanover, New Hampshire. The study is to proceed on the basis of the conjecture that every aspect of learning or any other feature of intelligence can in principle be so precisely described that a machine can be made to simulate it."

This statement encapsulates the audacious optimism and ambition that characterized the early days of AI. The participants believed that intelligence, in all its complexity, could be reduced to a set of computational processes that could be replicated by a machine.

Early AI Programs: Demonstrating the Potential

The Dartmouth workshop, while not producing any immediate earth-shattering breakthroughs *during the workshop itself*, served as a crucial catalyst for AI research. It established a common vocabulary, fostered collaboration among researchers from diverse backgrounds, and solidified the field's identity. Following the workshop, and in some cases based on ideas discussed there, several significant early AI programs emerged, demonstrating the potential of the field:

- **The Logic Theorist (1956):** Developed by Allen Newell and Herbert Simon at the RAND Corporation, the Logic Theorist was one of the first programs designed to simulate human problem-solving. It was capable of proving mathematical theorems from Bertrand Russell and Alfred North Whitehead's *Principia Mathematica*. This achievement was significant because it demonstrated that machines could perform tasks that were previously thought to require human ingenuity and logical reasoning.

- **General Problem Solver (GPS) (1957):** Also developed by Newell and Simon, the GPS was a more ambitious program designed to solve a wider range of problems using heuristic search methods. It attempted to simulate human problem-solving strategies by breaking down complex problems into smaller subproblems and applying general rules to find solutions. While the GPS had limitations, it introduced important concepts in AI, such as means-ends analysis and problem representation.

- **Checkers Player (1959):** Arthur Samuel at IBM developed a checkers-playing program that was able to learn and improve its performance over time. This program was a significant early example of machine learning, demonstrating that machines could learn from experience and adapt their strategies. Samuel's program eventually became proficient enough to beat a human checkers champion, further fueling the excitement surrounding AI.

The Rise of Symbolic AI: Focusing on Logic and Rules

These early programs largely relied on symbolic AI, an approach that focuses on representing knowledge using symbols and rules. This approach draws inspiration from formal logic and the idea that human thought can be reduced to the manipulation of symbols according to predefined rules. LISP (List Processing), a programming language developed by John McCarthy in 1958, became the dominant language for symbolic AI research due to its ability to easily manipulate symbolic data structures.

Early Optimism and the Challenges Ahead

The early years of AI were marked by a strong sense of optimism. Researchers believed that human-level artificial intelligence was just around the corner. They made bold predictions about the future of AI, envisioning machines that could solve any problem, understand natural language, and even exhibit consciousness.

However, the challenges of creating truly intelligent machines proved to be far greater than initially anticipated. The limitations of symbolic AI, the difficulty of representing real-world knowledge, and the computational limitations of the time would eventually lead to a period of disillusionment known as the "AI Winter," which we will explore in a later chapter.

Chapter 5: The Golden Age of AI: Expert Systems and the Pursuit of Intelligent Machines (1960s-Early 1970s)

The period spanning the 1960s and early 1970s is often referred to as the "Golden Age" of AI. Buoyed by the initial success of early AI programs and substantial funding from government agencies like the Advanced Research Projects Agency (ARPA, later DARPA), the field experienced a surge of research activity and optimism. This era was characterized by a focus on symbolic AI, with a particular emphasis on developing expert systems and exploring natural language processing, robotics, and early forms of machine learning. However, the limitations of the core programming languages of the time, LISP and Prolog, such as difficulty with real-time processing and limited ability to handle uncertainty, began to become apparent, foreshadowing future challenges.

Expert Systems: Capturing Human Expertise

One of the most promising areas of AI research during this period was the development of expert systems. These programs were designed to mimic the decision-making abilities of human experts in specific domains. By encoding knowledge in the form of rules and facts, expert systems could provide advice, diagnoses, and solutions to complex problems.

Several notable expert systems emerged during this era:

- **DENDRAL (1965):** Developed at Stanford University by Edward Feigenbaum, Joshua Lederberg, and Bruce Buchanan, DENDRAL was designed to analyze chemical compounds and infer their molecular structure based on mass spectrometry data. It was one of the earliest and most successful expert systems, demonstrating the potential of AI in scientific discovery. DENDRAL's success was due in part to its narrow, well-defined domain.

- **MYCIN (Early 1970s):** Also developed at Stanford, MYCIN was designed to diagnose bacterial infections and recommend appropriate antibiotic treatments. It was notable for its use of uncertainty factors to handle incomplete or uncertain information, a crucial aspect of medical diagnosis. MYCIN achieved a level of diagnostic accuracy comparable to human experts in some cases, showcasing the potential of AI in medical decision-making.

- **MACSYMA (Late 1960s-Early 1970s):** Developed at MIT, MACSYMA was a symbolic manipulation program capable of performing complex mathematical operations, such as integration, differentiation, and algebraic simplification. It was a powerful tool for scientists and engineers, demonstrating the potential of AI in automating complex mathematical tasks.

These expert systems demonstrated the potential of AI to solve real-world problems in specific domains. They captured human expertise in a computational form, making it accessible to non-experts and enabling faster and more consistent decision-making. However, the process of transferring human expertise into the systems proved to be a bottleneck, requiring significant time and effort from knowledge engineers.

Natural Language Processing: Communicating with Machines

Another significant area of research during the Golden Age was natural language processing (NLP). Researchers aimed to develop programs that could understand and generate human language, enabling more natural and intuitive human-computer interaction.

Early NLP systems employed various techniques, including parsing, semantic analysis, and knowledge representation. SHRDLU, developed by Terry Winograd at MIT in the late 1960s, was a notable example. SHRDLU operated in a simplified "blocks world," where it could understand and respond to natural language commands about the manipulation of blocks on a virtual table. While limited in its scope, SHRDLU demonstrated the potential of AI to understand and respond to human language in a constrained domain.

Robotics and Early Machine Learning

Robotics research also saw progress during this period. Shakey the Robot, developed at the Stanford Research Institute (SRI), was a pioneering example of an autonomous mobile robot. Shakey could perceive its environment using cameras and other sensors, create internal maps, and plan and execute actions to navigate its surroundings. Shakey used STRIPS (Stanford Research Institute Problem Solver), a planning algorithm, to determine the best sequence of actions to achieve its goals. While slow and limited in its capabilities by today's standards, Shakey represented a significant step towards creating robots that could interact intelligently with the physical world.

Early forms of machine learning, particularly work on perceptrons and other neural network models, also took place during this era. However, as we will discuss in the next chapter, a critical analysis of perceptrons by Marvin Minsky and Seymour Papert would contribute to the onset of the first "AI Winter."

The Limits of Early AI and the Seeds of Disillusionment

Despite the significant progress made during the Golden Age, several fundamental challenges began to emerge. Expert systems, while successful in narrow domains, proved difficult to scale to more complex real-world problems. The process of knowledge acquisition—eliciting and encoding knowledge from human experts—became a major bottleneck. Furthermore, these systems lacked common sense reasoning and the ability to generalize their knowledge to new situations. The limitations of the programming languages used, LISP and Prolog, also played a role, as they struggled with real-time processing and handling uncertainty inherent in real-world problems.

Similarly, early NLP systems struggled with ambiguity and context in human language. SHRDLU's success was limited to its simplified blocks world, and it could not handle more complex or open-ended conversations.

These limitations, combined with overly optimistic predictions about the near-term arrival of human-level AI, set the stage for a period of disillusionment and decreased funding, known as the AI Winter.

Chapter 6: The AI Winter: A Period of Disillusionment and Reassessment (Late 1970s-Mid 1980s)

The initial exuberance and optimism of the Golden Age of AI gave way to a period of disillusionment and reduced funding in the late 1970s and mid-1980s, often referred to as the "AI Winter." This period was marked by a growing realization that the challenges of creating truly intelligent machines were far more complex than initially anticipated. The limitations of the dominant approach of the time, symbolic AI, became increasingly apparent, leading to a decline in research funding and a reassessment of the field's direction.

The Lighthill Report: A Critical Assessment

One of the key events that contributed to the onset of the AI Winter was the publication of the Lighthill Report in 1973. Commissioned by the British government, the report, authored by Sir James Lighthill, provided a critical assessment of the state of AI research. Lighthill argued that AI had failed to deliver on its early promises and that many of the claims made by AI researchers were overly optimistic and lacked solid evidence.

The report highlighted several key criticisms:

- **Combinatorial Explosion:** Lighthill pointed out that many AI problems suffered from a "combinatorial explosion," meaning that the number of possible solutions grew exponentially with the size of the problem. This made it computationally infeasible to solve complex problems using brute-force search methods. For example, in planning a route for a robot through a complex environment, the number of possible paths could become astronomically large, making it impossible to explore all options.

- **Lack of Real-World Applicability:** The report argued that many AI programs were limited to toy problems and lacked the ability to generalize to real-world situations. Expert systems, while successful in narrow domains like diagnosing bacterial infections (MYCIN), proved difficult to scale to more complex problems like general medical diagnosis.

- **Focus on Toy Problems:** Lighthill criticized the field's focus on solving simple problems in constrained environments rather than tackling more complex and realistic challenges. For instance, SHRDLU, while impressive in its "blocks world," could not handle the complexities of natural language in real-world conversations.

The Lighthill Report had a significant impact on AI funding in the UK and other countries, contributing to a decline in research support and a general sense of disillusionment with the field.

The "Perceptrons" Critique: A Setback for Neural Networks

Another significant factor contributing to the AI Winter was the publication of Marvin Minsky and Seymour Papert's book *Perceptrons* in 1969. While the book itself was published in 1969, its major impact on funding and research trends occurred in the 1970s, aligning with the beginning of the AI Winter. *Perceptrons* provided a rigorous mathematical analysis of single-layer perceptrons, early neural network models.

Minsky and Papert showed that single-layer perceptrons could not solve certain types of problems, such as the XOR problem, which requires a non-linear decision boundary. This critique was widely interpreted as demonstrating the inherent limitations of *all* neural networks, leading to a significant decline in research funding for this approach. It's important to note that Minsky and Papert did *not* claim that *all* neural networks were incapable of solving such problems; their critique focused specifically on single-layer perceptrons. However, the nuance was often lost in the interpretation of their work.

The Limitations of Symbolic AI: Knowledge Representation and Common Sense

Beyond these specific critiques, the AI Winter also stemmed from the inherent limitations of the dominant approach of the time: symbolic AI. Representing real-world knowledge in a formal, symbolic form proved to be extremely difficult. The process of knowledge acquisition—eliciting and encoding knowledge from human experts—became a major bottleneck. Furthermore, symbolic AI systems lacked common sense reasoning and the ability to handle uncertainty and ambiguity, which are crucial aspects of human intelligence.

For example, early natural language processing systems struggled with the complexities of human language, such as ambiguity, context, and metaphor. These systems often relied on rigid rules and lacked the ability to understand the nuances of human communication. One example of a project that suffered due to these limitations was the early machine translation efforts, which struggled to produce accurate and fluent translations due to the complexity of language and the difficulty of encoding all the necessary rules and exceptions.

A Period of Reassessment and New Directions

Despite the challenges and reduced funding, the AI Winter was not a period of complete stagnation. While mainstream AI research focused less on grand claims of achieving human-level intelligence, important work continued in smaller pockets. This period of reassessment led to the development of new approaches and techniques that would eventually contribute to the resurgence of AI in later decades.

Some key developments during this period included:

- **Expert Systems Refinement:** While facing limitations, work on expert systems continued, leading to more robust and practical applications in specific domains. For example, work on rule-based systems for specific industrial control applications continued, albeit with less fanfare.

- **Focus on Knowledge Representation:** Research on knowledge representation techniques continued, exploring new ways to encode and organize knowledge in computational systems, such as semantic networks and frame-based systems.

- **Early Work on Machine Learning:** While neural network research declined, other areas of machine learning, such as inductive learning and decision trees, continued to be explored. This included work on algorithms like ID3 for decision tree learning.

The AI Winter, while a period of disillusionment and reduced funding, was a necessary period of reflection and reassessment. It forced the AI community to confront the limitations of existing approaches and paved the way for new ideas and techniques that would eventually lead to the next wave of AI innovation.

Chapter 7: The Connectionist Revolution: A Resurgence of Neural Networks (Mid-1980s-Early 1990s)

Following the AI Winter, a new approach to artificial intelligence began to gain momentum: connectionism. Inspired by the structure and function of the human brain, connectionist research focused on developing artificial neural networks, interconnected networks of simple processing units (neurons) that could learn from data. This approach offered a departure from the symbolic AI paradigm that had dominated the field in previous decades and laid the groundwork for the modern era of deep learning.

The Re-emergence of Neural Networks: Overcoming Past Limitations

While neural network research had suffered a setback due to the critique presented in Minsky and Papert's *Perceptrons*, work continued in smaller research communities. Several key developments helped to overcome some of the limitations of earlier models and paved the way for the resurgence of neural networks.

One crucial breakthrough was the development and popularization of the **backpropagation algorithm** in the mid-1980s. While the basic idea of backpropagation had been around for some time (with earlier work by Paul Werbos and others), its effective application to multi-layer neural networks was a significant advancement. Backpropagation provided a way to efficiently train these networks by calculating the error at the output layer and propagating it back through the network to adjust the connections (weights) between neurons. This allowed neural networks to learn more complex patterns and solve problems that were previously intractable, overcoming the limitations that Minsky and Papert had highlighted for single-layer perceptrons.

Another important development was the exploration of different network architectures, such as **recurrent neural networks (RNNs)**, which are particularly well-suited for processing sequential data like time series and natural language. RNNs have feedback connections that allow them to maintain a "memory" of past inputs, making them capable of capturing temporal dependencies in data. However, standard RNNs suffered from the **vanishing gradient problem**, where the gradients used to update the network's weights during training would become very small as they were propagated back through many time steps, hindering the network's ability to learn long-range dependencies.

Key Figures and Research: Laying the Foundation for Deep Learning

Several key figures played a crucial role in the connectionist revolution:

- **Geoffrey Hinton:** Hinton, along with David Rumelhart and Ronald Williams, played a pivotal role in popularizing backpropagation and demonstrating its effectiveness in training multi-layer neural networks. Their influential 1986 paper in *Nature* is often credited with reigniting interest in neural networks. Their work at the University of Toronto and Carnegie Mellon University helped to establish a solid theoretical and practical foundation.

- **Yann LeCun:** LeCun's work focused on developing convolutional neural networks (CNNs), a specialized type of neural network particularly effective for image recognition tasks. His work at Bell Labs and later at NYU demonstrated the potential of CNNs to learn hierarchical representations of visual data, using techniques like convolutional layers and pooling.

- **John Hopfield:** Hopfield's work on Hopfield networks, a type of recurrent neural network, contributed to the understanding of how neural networks could store and retrieve memories. These networks provided insights into associative memory and pattern completion.

These researchers and others helped to establish a solid theoretical and practical foundation for neural network research, paving the way for the breakthroughs that would follow in later decades.

Early Applications and Renewed Interest

The development of backpropagation and other advancements led to renewed interest in neural networks and a growing number of applications. Neural networks were successfully applied to various tasks, including:

- **Handwritten Character Recognition:** Neural networks achieved significant success in recognizing handwritten characters, a task with practical applications in postal sorting and other areas. Yann LeCun's work on CNNs was particularly influential in this domain.

- **Speech Recognition:** Early speech recognition systems based on neural networks began to show promise, laying the groundwork for the voice assistants and other speech-based technologies we use today.

- **Financial Modeling:** Neural networks were used in financial applications for tasks such as stock market prediction and fraud detection, although with varying degrees of success.

These successes helped to demonstrate the practical potential of neural networks and contributed to a resurgence of funding and research activity in the field.

From Connectionism to Deep Learning: The Next Step

While the connectionist revolution marked a significant step forward, it was still limited by the computational resources available at the time and the size of the datasets that could be used to train neural networks. The networks of this era were relatively shallow, with only a few layers of neurons. The next major breakthrough, the rise of deep learning, would require significantly more computational power and larger datasets, which would become available with the advent of the Big Data revolution and advancements in hardware like GPUs. Furthermore, addressing the vanishing gradient problem in RNNs more effectively would be key for the development of more sophisticated sequence models.

Chapter 8: The Rise of Machine Learning: From Rules to Data (Late 1980s-2000s)

While connectionism and neural networks experienced a resurgence, the late 1980s and the 1990s also saw significant advancements in other areas of artificial intelligence, collectively known as machine learning. This period marked a crucial shift from explicitly programming rules and knowledge into AI systems to developing algorithms that could learn patterns and make predictions directly from data. This data-driven approach proved to be highly effective in a wide range of applications and laid the groundwork for the deep learning revolution that would follow.

The Shift to Data-Driven Approaches: Learning from Experience

The limitations of symbolic AI, particularly the difficulty of knowledge acquisition and the brittleness of rule-based systems, highlighted the need for alternative approaches. Machine learning offered a compelling solution: instead of manually encoding knowledge, researchers developed algorithms that could learn from data, automatically discovering patterns and relationships. This approach allowed AI systems to adapt to new situations and improve their performance over time, making them more robust and practical for real-world applications.

Key Paradigms of Machine Learning: Supervised, Unsupervised, and Reinforcement Learning

Three primary learning paradigms emerged within machine learning:

- **Supervised Learning:** In supervised learning, the algorithm learns from labeled data, where each input is paired with a corresponding output or label. The goal is to learn a mapping function that can predict the output for new, unseen inputs. Examples include:

- - - Image classification: Classifying images of cats and dogs.
  - Spam filtering: Identifying emails as spam or not spam.
  - Regression tasks: Predicting house prices based on features like size and location. Common algorithms include linear regression (for regression), logistic regression (for classification), support vector machines (SVMs), and decision trees.
- **Unsupervised Learning:** In unsupervised learning, the algorithm learns from unlabeled data, discovering hidden patterns and structures without explicit guidance. The goal is to find relationships, clusters, or anomalies in the data. Examples include:
  - **Customer segmentation:** Grouping customers based on purchasing behavior.
  - **Anomaly detection:** Identifying fraudulent transactions in financial data.
  - **Dimensionality reduction:** Reducing the number of variables in a dataset while preserving important information. Common algorithms include k-means clustering, principal component analysis (PCA), and association rule mining.
- **Reinforcement Learning:** In reinforcement learning, an agent learns to interact with an environment by taking actions and receiving rewards or penalties. The goal is to learn a policy that maximizes the cumulative reward over time. Examples include:
  - **Game playing:** Training an AI to play chess or Go.
  - **Robotics:** Training a robot to navigate a maze or manipulate objects.
  - **Control systems:** Optimizing the control of industrial processes. Key concepts include Markov Decision Processes (MDPs), Q-learning, and policy gradients.

Key Algorithms and Techniques: Expanding the Toolkit

Several key algorithms and techniques emerged during this period, significantly expanding the machine learning toolkit:

- **Support Vector Machines (SVMs):** SVMs are powerful supervised learning algorithms that find the optimal hyperplane to separate data points into different classes. They are particularly effective in high-dimensional spaces and have been successfully applied to various tasks, including image classification, text categorization, and bioinformatics.

- **Decision Trees:** Decision trees are tree-like structures that represent a set of rules for classifying data. They are easy to understand and interpret and can handle both categorical and numerical data. Random Forests, an ensemble learning method that combines multiple decision trees, further improved performance and robustness. The ID3 algorithm is a classic example of a decision tree learning algorithm.

- **Bayesian Networks:** Bayesian networks are probabilistic graphical models that represent the dependencies between variables. They are used for reasoning under uncertainty and have applications in areas such as medical diagnosis, spam filtering, and risk assessment.

- **Boosting:** Boosting algorithms combine multiple weak learners (e.g., simple decision trees) to create a strong learner. AdaBoost and Gradient Boosting are popular examples of boosting algorithms that have achieved state-of-the-art performance in various tasks.

Applications and Impact: Bringing Machine Learning to the Real World

The advancements in machine learning during this period led to a growing number of practical applications in various domains:

- **Data Mining:** Machine learning techniques were widely used for data mining, discovering hidden patterns and insights from large datasets in areas such as marketing (e.g., customer segmentation), finance (e.g., credit scoring), and retail (e.g., market basket analysis).

- **Bioinformatics:** Machine learning played a crucial role in analyzing genomic data, identifying disease markers, and developing new drugs. For example, machine learning algorithms were used to analyze gene expression data to identify potential drug targets for cancer.

- **Web Search:** Search engines began to incorporate machine learning algorithms to improve search relevance and personalize search results. This included techniques like PageRank, which used graph analysis and machine learning to rank web pages based on their importance and relevance.

Setting the Stage for Deep Learning: The Need for More Data and Computation

While machine learning proved to be highly effective in many applications, it still faced limitations. Many algorithms struggled to handle high-dimensional data and complex patterns. The next major breakthrough, deep learning, would require significantly more data and computational power to train larger and more complex neural networks. This would become possible with the rise of the Big Data revolution and advancements in hardware like GPUs, which we will explore in the next chapter. Furthermore, while effective, many machine learning algorithms of this era required careful feature engineering, a process of manually selecting and transforming relevant features from the data. Deep learning promised to automate this process, learning features directly from raw data.

Chapter 9: The Big Data Revolution: Fueling the AI Boom (2000s-2010s)

The early 2000s and 2010s witnessed an explosion of data, often referred to as the "Big Data revolution." This unprecedented growth in the volume, velocity, and variety of data, coupled with advancements in computing infrastructure and the increasing availability of open-source software, provided the fuel for the next major wave of AI innovation, particularly in the area of deep learning. This chapter explores the key factors that contributed to the Big Data revolution and its profound impact on the field of artificial intelligence.

The Explosion of Data: Volume, Velocity, and Variety

Several factors contributed to the dramatic increase in data generation during this period:

- **The Rise of the Internet and the World Wide Web:** The widespread adoption of the internet and the growth of the World Wide Web created vast amounts of data from online interactions, web pages, and digital content. Search engines like Google indexed billions of web pages, creating massive datasets of text and links.

- **Social Media Platforms:** The emergence of social media platforms like Facebook, Twitter, and YouTube generated massive amounts of user-generated content, including text, images, videos, and social interactions. These platforms became rich sources of data on user behavior, preferences, and social connections.

- **Mobile Devices and Sensors:** The proliferation of smartphones and other mobile devices equipped with various sensors (GPS, cameras, accelerometers) generated a constant stream of location data, images, videos, and other sensor readings. This data provided valuable insights into human mobility, behavior, and the physical world.

- **The Internet of Things (IoT):** The increasing connectivity of everyday objects, from appliances to cars, through the Internet of Things created a vast network of data-generating devices. This data provided opportunities for optimizing processes, predicting failures, and improving efficiency in various industries.

This explosion of data was characterized by three key dimensions, often referred to as the "three Vs":

- **Volume:** The sheer amount of data generated was unprecedented, with data volumes growing exponentially. This required new methods for storing and processing such massive datasets.

- **Velocity:** Data was generated and processed at an increasingly rapid pace, requiring new methods for real-time data analysis. For example, social media platforms generated millions of posts and comments every minute, requiring real-time analysis for trends and sentiment.

- **Variety:** Data came in various formats, including structured data (databases), unstructured data (text, images, videos), and semi-structured data (XML, JSON). This required new techniques for data integration and processing.

Advancements in Computing Infrastructure: Handling Massive Datasets

The Big Data revolution was enabled not only by the growth of data but also by significant advancements in computing infrastructure and the growing availability of open source software:

- **Cloud Computing:** The rise of cloud computing platforms like Amazon Web Services (AWS), Google Cloud Platform (GCP), and Microsoft Azure provided access to scalable and affordable computing resources, allowing researchers and companies to process and store massive datasets without investing in expensive hardware infrastructure.

- **Distributed Computing:** Distributed computing frameworks like Hadoop and Apache Spark, often available as open-source software, enabled the parallel processing of large datasets across clusters of computers, significantly speeding up data analysis and model training. This made it possible to process datasets that were previously too large to handle on a single machine.

- **Graphical Processing Units (GPUs):** GPUs, originally designed for graphics rendering, proved to be highly effective for accelerating the computations involved in training neural networks, particularly deep learning models. Their parallel processing architecture allowed for much faster training times, making it possible to train larger and more complex models.

The Impact on AI: Fueling Deep Learning and Other Applications

The availability of massive datasets and powerful computing resources had a profound impact on the field of AI, particularly in the area of deep learning:

- **Training Larger and More Complex Models:** The availability of large datasets allowed researchers to train much larger and more complex neural networks, leading to significant improvements in performance on various tasks. For example, the ImageNet dataset, with millions of labeled images, played a crucial role in the development of deep learning for image recognition.

- **The Rise of Deep Learning:** Deep learning models, with their multiple layers of neurons, were able to learn hierarchical representations of data, capturing complex patterns and achieving state-of-the-art results in areas such as image recognition, natural language processing, and speech recognition.

- **New Applications and Opportunities:** The Big Data revolution opened up new opportunities for AI applications in various domains, including personalized recommendations (e.g., Netflix recommendations), fraud detection (e.g., credit card fraud), predictive maintenance (e.g., predicting equipment failures), and autonomous driving.

Data as the New Currency: The Rise of Data-Driven Companies

The ability to collect, process, and analyze large datasets became a key competitive advantage for companies in various industries. Companies like Google, Facebook, Amazon, and Netflix built their businesses on data-driven insights, using AI and machine learning to personalize user experiences, optimize operations, and develop new products and services. Data became the new currency, and the ability to extract value from data became a crucial skill for businesses in the digital age.

Ethical Considerations: Privacy, Bias, and Accountability

The Big Data revolution also raised important ethical considerations, particularly regarding privacy, bias, and accountability:

- **Privacy Concerns:** The collection and use of large amounts of personal data raised concerns about privacy and data security. For example, data breaches and the use of personal data for targeted advertising raised significant privacy concerns.

- **Bias in Data:** Machine learning models trained on biased data can perpetuate and amplify existing societal biases, leading to unfair or discriminatory outcomes.

- **Accountability and Transparency:** The complexity of some AI models made it difficult to understand how they made decisions, raising concerns about accountability and transparency.

These ethical considerations became increasingly important as AI systems were deployed in more critical applications, highlighting the need for responsible AI development and deployment.

Chapter 10: The Deep Learning Breakthrough: A New Era of AI (2010s-Present)

The convergence of the Big Data revolution, advancements in computing hardware (especially GPUs), and crucial algorithmic innovations led to a significant breakthrough in artificial intelligence: the rise of deep learning. Deep learning, a subfield of machine learning based on artificial neural networks with multiple layers (hence "deep"), achieved remarkable success in various domains, ushering in a new era of AI and transforming industries worldwide. However, it is also important to acknowledge the limitations of deep learning, such as its data hunger and lack of inherent interpretability, which continue to be areas of active research.

The Power of Deep Neural Networks: Learning Hierarchical Representations

Deep learning models, particularly deep neural networks, differ from traditional machine learning models in their ability to learn hierarchical representations of data. Each layer in a deep network learns increasingly abstract features from the input data, allowing the model to capture complex patterns and relationships. For example, in image recognition, the first layers might learn to detect edges and corners, while subsequent layers learn to recognize more complex features like shapes, objects, and eventually, entire scenes. This hierarchical learning allows deep learning models to automatically learn relevant features from raw data, reducing the need for manual feature engineering, a significant advantage over previous machine learning approaches.

This ability to learn hierarchical representations proved to be crucial for achieving state-of-the-art performance in various tasks, particularly those involving complex, unstructured data like images, text, and speech.

Key Architectural Innovations: CNNs and RNNs

Two key architectural innovations played a crucial role in the deep learning breakthrough:

- **Convolutional Neural Networks (CNNs):** CNNs are specifically designed for processing data with a grid-like topology, such as images. They use convolutional layers, which apply filters to small regions of the input data, allowing the network to learn local patterns and spatial hierarchies. CNNs achieved remarkable success in image recognition tasks, surpassing previous methods by a significant margin. For example, CNNs are used in image classification tasks to identify objects within an image, and in object detection tasks to locate and classify multiple objects within an image.
- **Recurrent Neural Networks (RNNs):** RNNs are designed for processing sequential data, such as time series and natural language. They have feedback connections that allow them to maintain a "memory" of past inputs, making them capable of capturing temporal dependencies in data. However, standard RNNs struggled with the

vanishing gradient problem, making it difficult to learn long-range dependencies. Variants of RNNs, such as Long Short-Term Memory (LSTM) networks and Gated Recurrent Units (GRUs), addressed this issue by introducing gating mechanisms that regulate the flow of information through the network, allowing them to learn long-range dependencies in sequences, making them suitable for tasks like machine translation and speech recognition.

The ImageNet Moment: A Paradigm Shift in Image Recognition

A pivotal moment in the deep learning revolution occurred in 2012 with the ImageNet Large Scale Visual Recognition Challenge (ILSVRC). Alex Krizhevsky, Ilya Sutskever, and Geoffrey Hinton, from the University of Toronto, introduced **AlexNet**, a deep convolutional neural network that significantly outperformed all previous competitors. AlexNet reduced the top-5 error rate by a substantial margin, demonstrating the power of deep learning for image recognition and triggering a surge of interest and investment in the field.

Key innovations in AlexNet included the use of ReLU activation functions, which accelerated training compared to traditional sigmoid functions, and the implementation of dropout, a regularization technique that prevented overfitting by randomly ignoring some neurons during training. This success reignited research into neural networks and ushered in the modern era of deep learning.

Natural Language Processing Breakthroughs: From Word Embeddings to Transformers

Deep learning also revolutionized natural language processing (NLP). The development of **word embeddings**, such as Word2Vec and GloVe, allowed words to be represented as dense vectors in a high-dimensional space, capturing semantic relationships between words. This enabled deep learning models to better understand the meaning of words and sentences.

More recently, the introduction of **transformer networks**, with their attention mechanisms, has led to even more significant breakthroughs in NLP. Transformer models, such as BERT (Bidirectional Encoder Representations from Transformers) and GPT (Generative Pre-trained Transformer), have achieved state-of-the-art results in various NLP tasks, including machine translation, text summarization, and question answering. These models use self-attention mechanisms to weigh the importance of different words in a sentence when processing it, allowing them to capture long-range dependencies and contextual information more effectively than previous models.

Key Applications and Impact: Transforming Industries

The deep learning breakthrough has had a profound impact on various industries and applications:

- **Image Recognition and Computer Vision:** Deep learning powers facial recognition systems, object detection in autonomous vehicles, and medical image analysis for tasks like detecting tumors in X-rays.

- **Natural Language Processing:** Deep learning enables virtual assistants like Siri and Alexa, machine translation tools, and sentiment analysis systems used for market research and social media monitoring.

- **Speech Recognition:** Deep learning has significantly improved the accuracy of speech recognition systems, enabling voice search, voice control, and transcription services used in various applications, from customer service to accessibility tools.

- **Drug Discovery and Healthcare:** Deep learning is used for drug discovery, disease diagnosis, and personalized medicine. For example, deep learning models are used to predict the efficacy of drug candidates and identify potential drug targets.

- **Finance and Fintech:** Deep learning is used for fraud detection, algorithmic trading, and risk assessment. For example, deep learning models can analyze financial transactions to identify patterns indicative of fraudulent activity.

The Ongoing Evolution of Deep Learning: New Architectures and Techniques

Deep learning continues to evolve rapidly, with ongoing research into new architectures, training techniques, and applications. Some key areas of current research include:

- **Generative Adversarial Networks (GANs):** GANs are used for generating synthetic data, such as images, text, and music. They consist of two neural networks, a generator and a discriminator, that are trained in a competitive manner.

- **Reinforcement Learning with Deep Neural Networks:** Combining reinforcement learning with deep learning has led to breakthroughs in game playing (e.g., AlphaGo, which defeated human Go champions) and robotics.

- **Explainable AI (XAI):** Research on XAI aims to develop methods for making deep learning models more transparent and interpretable, addressing the "black box" problem and improving trust in AI systems.

Part III: The Future and Legacy of AI

Chapter 11: AI in Action: Transforming Industries and Everyday Life (2010s-Present)

The deep learning revolution, fueled by Big Data and advanced computing, transitioned AI from a primarily research-driven field to a powerful force transforming industries and impacting everyday life. This chapter explores the diverse applications of AI across various sectors, showcasing its real-world impact and its integration into our daily routines. It also touches upon some of the industry-specific ethical considerations that arise with these applications.

Healthcare: Revolutionizing Diagnosis, Treatment, and Drug Discovery

AI is revolutionizing healthcare in several ways:

- **Medical Imaging Analysis:** Deep learning models are used to analyze medical images (X-rays, CT scans, MRIs) with increasing accuracy, assisting radiologists in detecting diseases like cancer, Alzheimer's, and other conditions. This leads to earlier diagnosis and more effective treatment. However, ethical concerns arise regarding data privacy, algorithmic bias potentially leading to misdiagnosis in certain demographic groups, and the potential for over-reliance on AI systems.

- **Drug Discovery and Development:** AI accelerates the process of drug discovery by analyzing vast amounts of biological data, predicting the effectiveness of drug candidates, and identifying potential drug targets. This significantly reduces the time and cost associated with developing new treatments. Ethical considerations include ensuring fairness and transparency in drug development processes and preventing the misuse of AI for developing harmful biological agents.

- **Personalized Medicine:** AI is used to analyze patient data, including genetic information, lifestyle factors, and medical history, to develop personalized treatment plans tailored to individual needs. Ethical concerns include data privacy, ensuring equitable access to personalized medicine, and the potential for genetic discrimination.

- **Robotic Surgery:** AI-powered robots are used in surgical procedures to enhance precision, minimize invasiveness, and improve patient outcomes. Ethical concerns center around the safety and reliability of these systems, the potential for technical malfunctions, and the need for adequate human oversight.

Transportation: The Rise of Autonomous Vehicles

The development of self-driving cars, powered by sophisticated AI algorithms, is poised to revolutionize transportation:

- **Autonomous Navigation:** AI algorithms use sensor data (cameras, lidar, radar) to perceive the environment, navigate roads, and make driving decisions without human intervention. Ethical dilemmas arise around accident responsibility ("the trolley problem"), the potential for job displacement for professional drivers, and the security of these systems against hacking and malicious attacks.

- **Traffic Optimization:** AI can be used to optimize traffic flow, reduce congestion, and improve fuel efficiency. However, ethical considerations include ensuring fairness in traffic management and avoiding discriminatory impacts on certain communities.

- **Logistics and Delivery:** AI-powered robots and drones are being developed for package delivery and logistics, automating supply chains and improving efficiency. Ethical considerations include the impact on employment in the delivery sector and the potential for privacy violations through drone surveillance.

Finance and Fintech: Automating Processes and Detecting Fraud

AI is transforming the financial industry in various ways:

- **Fraud Detection:** Machine learning algorithms are used to detect fraudulent transactions in real-time, protecting businesses and consumers from financial losses. Ethical concerns include ensuring fairness and avoiding bias in fraud detection algorithms, which could disproportionately target certain demographic groups.

- **Algorithmic Trading:** AI-powered trading systems automate investment decisions, analyzing market data and executing trades at high speeds. Ethical concerns include the potential for market manipulation, the creation of "flash crashes," and the exacerbation of existing financial inequalities.

- **Risk Assessment:** AI is used to assess credit risk, predict loan defaults, and manage financial risk. Ethical concerns include ensuring fairness and avoiding bias in credit scoring algorithms, which could perpetuate discriminatory lending practices.

- **Personalized Financial Advice:** AI-powered chatbots and virtual assistants provide personalized financial advice to customers. Ethical concerns include ensuring the accuracy and reliability of this advice and protecting consumers from misleading or harmful recommendations.

Retail and E-commerce: Personalizing the Customer Experience

AI is used in retail and e-commerce to enhance the customer experience and optimize business operations:

- **Personalized Recommendations:** Recommendation systems use AI to suggest products and services to customers based on their browsing history, purchase behavior, and preferences. Ethical concerns include the creation of "filter bubbles" that limit exposure to diverse perspectives and the potential for manipulative marketing tactics.

- **Chatbots and Virtual Assistants:** AI-powered chatbots provide customer support, answer questions, and assist with purchases. Ethical concerns include ensuring data privacy and preventing the misuse of customer data.

- **Supply Chain Optimization:** AI is used to optimize inventory management, predict demand, and streamline logistics. Ethical considerations include the impact on employment in the retail and logistics sectors.

Entertainment and Media: Creating and Distributing Content

AI is also impacting the entertainment and media industry:

- **Content Creation:** AI is used to generate music, write scripts, and create visual effects. Ethical concerns include questions of authorship and copyright, the potential for AI to create deepfakes and misinformation, and the impact on human artists and creators.

- **Personalized Recommendations:** Streaming services use AI to recommend movies, TV shows, and music to users. Ethical concerns include the creation of filter bubbles and the potential for biased recommendations that reinforce existing stereotypes.

- **Content Moderation:** AI is used to moderate online content, detecting hate speech, misinformation, and other harmful content. Ethical concerns include the accuracy of AI moderation systems, the potential for censorship, and the impact on freedom of speech.

Everyday AI: Virtual Assistants and Smart Devices

AI has become increasingly integrated into our daily lives through virtual assistants and smart devices:

- **Virtual Assistants:** Virtual assistants like Siri, Alexa, and Google Assistant use natural language processing and machine learning to understand voice commands, answer questions, and perform tasks. Ethical concerns include data privacy, the potential for these devices to eavesdrop on conversations, and the impact on human social interaction.

- **Smart Home Devices:** Smart home devices use AI to automate tasks, control appliances, and personalize home environments. Ethical concerns include data privacy, the security of these devices against hacking, and the potential for these devices to be used for surveillance.

- **Personalized Recommendations:** Social media platforms, streaming services, and e-commerce websites use AI to provide personalized recommendations. Ethical concerns include the creation of filter bubbles and the manipulation of user behavior through targeted advertising.

The Pervasiveness of AI: A Transforming Force

AI is no longer a futuristic concept; it is a pervasive force transforming industries and impacting our daily lives. From healthcare to transportation, finance to entertainment, AI is automating tasks, improving efficiency, and creating new possibilities. However, this widespread adoption also raises important ethical and societal considerations, which require careful attention and proactive solutions.

Chapter 12: The Challenges and Opportunities of AI: Ethical, Societal, and Economic Implications

The rapid advancement and widespread adoption of AI bring not only immense opportunities but also significant challenges. This chapter explores the key ethical, societal, and economic implications of AI, highlighting the need for responsible development and deployment of this powerful technology.

Ethical Considerations: Bias, Fairness, Accountability, and Transparency

One of the most pressing concerns surrounding AI is the potential for bias in algorithms. AI systems learn from data, and if that data reflects existing societal biases, the AI system will likely perpetuate and even amplify those biases. This can lead to unfair or discriminatory outcomes in various applications:

- **Bias in Facial Recognition:** Facial recognition systems have been shown to be less accurate for people with darker skin tones, leading to potential misidentification and wrongful arrests. For example, studies have shown that some commercially available facial recognition systems have significantly higher error rates for darker-skinned individuals, particularly women. This can have severe consequences in law enforcement and security contexts.

- **Bias in Hiring Algorithms:** AI-powered hiring tools can perpetuate gender or racial biases if the training data reflects historical biases in hiring practices. For instance, if a company's historical hiring data shows a preference for male applicants, an AI system trained on this data will likely reproduce this bias, even if unintentional.

- **Bias in Loan Applications:** AI systems used for loan approvals can discriminate against certain demographic groups if the training data reflects historical lending disparities. For example, if historical data shows that people living in certain neighborhoods are less likely to be approved for loans, an AI system trained on this data may unfairly deny loans to applicants from those neighborhoods, even if they are financially qualified. The COMPAS (Correctional Offender Management Profiling for Alternative Sanctions) algorithm, used in the US justice system to assess recidivism risk, is a well-known example of algorithmic bias, showing disparities in risk assessment for different racial groups.

Addressing bias in AI requires careful attention to data collection, algorithm design, and evaluation. It is crucial to ensure that training data is representative of the population and that algorithms are designed to be fair and unbiased. Techniques like data augmentation, bias detection algorithms, and fairness-aware machine learning can help mitigate bias.

Another important ethical consideration is accountability. When an AI system makes a mistake or causes harm, it can be difficult to determine who is responsible. Is it the programmer? The data scientist? The company that deployed the system? Establishing clear lines of accountability is crucial for ensuring responsible AI development and deployment. This is particularly relevant in high-stakes applications like autonomous vehicles, where an accident caused by an AI system raises complex legal and ethical questions about liability.

Transparency is also essential. Many deep learning models are "black boxes," meaning that it is difficult to understand how they arrive at their decisions. This lack of transparency can make it difficult to identify and correct biases or errors in the system. Research in Explainable AI (XAI) aims to develop methods for making AI models more transparent and interpretable, allowing for better understanding and accountability.

Societal Impacts: Job Displacement, Inequality, and Surveillance

The increasing automation capabilities of AI raise concerns about job displacement. As AI systems become more sophisticated, they can automate tasks that were previously performed by humans, potentially leading to job losses in various sectors. This can exacerbate existing inequalities and create new social challenges. For example, the automation of manufacturing processes has already led to job losses in the manufacturing sector, and the increasing capabilities of AI in areas like customer service and data entry could lead to further job displacement in the service sector.

The widespread use of AI for surveillance also raises significant societal concerns. Facial recognition systems, coupled with large databases of personal information, can be used for mass surveillance, eroding privacy and civil liberties. The use of AI-powered surveillance systems in public spaces raises concerns about potential misuse by governments and law enforcement agencies.

Economic Implications: Productivity, Innovation, and the Future of Work

AI has the potential to significantly boost productivity and drive innovation across various industries. By automating tasks, optimizing processes, and generating new insights from data, AI can create new economic opportunities and improve efficiency. For example, AI-powered optimization algorithms can improve supply chain efficiency, reduce energy consumption, and optimize manufacturing processes.

However, the economic benefits of AI may not be distributed equally. The potential for job displacement and the concentration of AI expertise in a few companies could exacerbate existing inequalities. It is crucial to implement policies that mitigate the negative economic impacts of AI and ensure that the benefits are shared more broadly. This might include investing in retraining programs for displaced workers, exploring new economic models like universal basic income, and promoting greater access to AI education and training.

Opportunities: Augmenting Human Capabilities and Solving Global Challenges

Despite the challenges, AI also offers tremendous opportunities to augment human capabilities and address some of the world's most pressing challenges:

- **Augmented Intelligence:** AI can enhance human capabilities by providing tools and insights that amplify human intelligence. This can lead to improved decision-making, increased productivity, and new forms of creativity. For example, AI-powered tools can assist doctors in diagnosing diseases, scientists in analyzing complex data, and artists in creating new forms of art.
- **Solving Global Challenges:** AI can be used to address global challenges such as climate change, poverty, and disease. For example, AI can be used to optimize energy consumption, develop new treatments for diseases, and improve agricultural productivity.

The Need for Responsible AI Development and Deployment

Addressing the challenges and realizing the opportunities of AI requires a concerted effort from researchers, policymakers, and the public. It is crucial to develop and deploy AI in a responsible and ethical manner, ensuring that it benefits humanity as a whole. This includes:

- **Developing ethical guidelines and standards for AI development.**
- **Promoting transparency and accountability in AI systems.**
- **Investing in education and training to prepare the workforce for the changing job market.**
- **Engaging in public discourse about the societal implications of AI.**

By addressing these challenges and embracing the opportunities, we can ensure that AI is used to create a better future for all.

Chapter 13: The Future of Human-AI Collaboration: Augmented Intelligence and the Quest for AGI

The future of artificial intelligence is not simply about creating machines that can replace humans. A more compelling and productive vision is one of human-AI collaboration, where AI augments human capabilities, allowing us to achieve more than we could alone. This chapter explores the concept of augmented intelligence, the ongoing pursuit of Artificial General Intelligence (AGI), and the potential future directions of human-AI interaction, including the philosophical implications of achieving AGI.

Augmented Intelligence: Enhancing Human Capabilities

Augmented intelligence, sometimes referred to as "intelligence augmentation" or "IA," focuses on using AI to enhance human cognitive abilities rather than replacing them. This approach emphasizes the complementary strengths of humans and AI: humans excel at creativity, critical thinking, emotional intelligence, and complex social interactions, while AI excels at processing large amounts of data, identifying patterns, performing repetitive tasks, and operating with speed and precision.

Examples of augmented intelligence in practice include:

- **AI-powered decision support systems:** These systems provide insights and recommendations to human decision-makers in various fields, such as healthcare (e.g., AI assisting doctors with diagnoses and treatment planning), finance (e.g., AI providing insights for investment strategies), and business (e.g., AI optimizing supply chains and marketing campaigns). By analyzing large datasets and identifying relevant patterns, these systems can help humans make more informed and effective decisions.

- **AI-assisted design and engineering:** AI tools can assist designers and engineers in creating new products and optimizing existing ones. These tools can generate design options, simulate performance, and identify potential problems, allowing humans to focus on the creative and strategic aspects of the design process. For instance, AI can generate multiple architectural designs based on specific constraints, allowing human architects to select and refine the most promising options.

- **AI-powered learning platforms:** These platforms personalize learning experiences for individual students, adapting to their learning styles and providing customized feedback. This can lead to more effective learning outcomes and greater student engagement. AI tutors can provide personalized instruction and feedback, adapting to each student's pace and learning style.

- **AI for accessibility:** AI-powered tools can enhance accessibility for people with disabilities. For example, AI-powered speech-to-text and text-to-speech technologies can help people with visual or auditory impairments communicate more effectively. AI can also be used to develop assistive technologies for people with motor impairments, such as AI-powered wheelchairs and robotic prosthetics.

Augmented intelligence represents a powerful paradigm for human-AI collaboration, enabling us to leverage the strengths of both humans and machines to achieve greater things and solve complex problems that neither could tackle alone.

The Quest for Artificial General Intelligence (AGI): Towards Human-Level AI

While augmented intelligence focuses on enhancing specific human capabilities, the long-term goal of some AI researchers is to achieve Artificial General Intelligence (AGI), also known as "strong AI." AGI refers to a hypothetical AI system with human-level general intelligence, capable of performing any intellectual task that a human being can.

Achieving AGI remains a significant challenge, and there is no consensus on how to achieve it. Some of the key challenges include:

- **Understanding Consciousness and Sentience:** We still lack a complete understanding of human consciousness and sentience, making it difficult to replicate these qualities in machines. This raises philosophical questions about whether consciousness can even be replicated in a non-biological substrate.

- **Common Sense Reasoning:** AGI systems would need to possess common sense reasoning, the ability to understand and reason about the everyday world in the same way that humans do. This is a complex problem that requires representing vast amounts of implicit knowledge about the world.

- **Transfer Learning and Generalization:** AGI systems would need to be able to transfer knowledge learned in one domain to other domains and generalize their knowledge to new situations. This is a key aspect of human intelligence that is difficult to replicate in machines.

Despite these challenges, research on AGI continues, with various approaches being explored, including:

- **Neuro-inspired AI:** This approach draws inspiration from the structure and function of the human brain, attempting to build AI systems that more closely mimic biological intelligence.

- **Evolutionary Algorithms:** These algorithms use principles of natural selection to evolve AI systems over time, gradually improving their performance.

- **Hybrid Approaches:** These approaches combine different AI techniques, such as symbolic AI, connectionism, and machine learning, to create more powerful and versatile systems.

The Future of Human-AI Interaction: A Symbiotic Relationship and Philosophical Implications

The future of human-AI interaction is likely to be characterized by a symbiotic relationship, where humans and AI work together seamlessly to achieve common goals. This could involve:

- **Intelligent Personal Assistants:** Advanced virtual assistants that can anticipate our needs, manage our schedules, and provide personalized information and support, becoming true partners in our daily lives.

- **AI-powered collaboration tools:** Tools that facilitate collaboration between humans and AI in various domains, such as scientific research, creative arts, and business, accelerating discovery and innovation.
- **Brain-Computer Interfaces (BCIs):** Technologies that allow direct communication between the human brain and computers, potentially enabling even more seamless integration with AI systems, blurring the lines between human and machine intelligence.

The achievement of AGI, if it occurs, would have profound philosophical implications. It would challenge our understanding of consciousness, intelligence, and what it means to be human. It would raise questions about the rights and responsibilities of intelligent machines and their place in society. Some of the key philosophical questions that arise include:

- **What is the nature of consciousness, and can it be replicated in a machine?**
- **If a machine is conscious, does it have rights?**
- **How would the existence of AGI impact our understanding of humanity's place in the universe?**

The future of human-AI collaboration holds immense potential for transforming our lives and solving some of the world's most pressing challenges. However, it is crucial to approach this future with careful consideration of the ethical and societal implications, ensuring that AI is used to benefit humanity as a whole. The pursuit of AGI, in particular, requires careful consideration of its potential impact on the human condition.

Chapter 14: The Legacy of AI: A Continuing Quest to Understand Intelligence

The story of artificial intelligence is more than just a chronicle of technological advancements; it's a profound exploration of intelligence itself. From ancient myths of artificial beings to today's sophisticated algorithms, the pursuit of AI has driven us to confront fundamental questions about the nature of thought, consciousness, and what it means to be intelligent. This chapter reflects on the legacy of AI, its impact on our understanding of intelligence, its continuing influence on our world, and the current state of the field.

A Mirror to Ourselves: Understanding Human Cognition

The quest to create artificial intelligence has inadvertently served as a mirror to ourselves, forcing us to examine the intricacies of human cognition. In attempting to replicate human intelligence in machines, we have gained deeper insights into how we think, learn, and perceive the world.

Early AI research, focused on symbolic AI and logic, highlighted the importance of knowledge representation and reasoning. The challenges encountered in encoding common sense knowledge and handling uncertainty revealed the limitations of purely rule-based approaches and underscored the importance of learning and adaptation.

The connectionist revolution, with its focus on neural networks, drew inspiration from the structure and function of the human brain, leading to a better understanding of how information is processed and represented in biological systems. The success of deep learning, with its ability to learn hierarchical representations from data, further illuminated the power of learning from experience and the importance of data in shaping intelligence. By trying to build artificial minds, we have gained valuable insights into how our own minds work.

A Catalyst for Technological Innovation: Transforming Industries and Society

AI has not only advanced our understanding of intelligence but has also served as a powerful catalyst for technological innovation, transforming industries and reshaping society. From healthcare to transportation, finance to entertainment, AI is automating tasks, improving efficiency, and creating new possibilities.

The development of AI has spurred advancements in various related fields, including computer science, mathematics, neuroscience, cognitive science, and even fields like linguistics and psychology. It has also led to the creation of new industries and job opportunities, driving economic growth and innovation. AI has become an integral part of the digital economy, impacting everything from online search and e-commerce to social media and entertainment.

A Continuing Dialogue: Ethical and Societal Implications

The development and deployment of AI have also sparked important ethical and societal debates. Concerns about bias, fairness, accountability, transparency, job displacement, and privacy have highlighted the need for responsible AI development and deployment.

These debates have fostered a crucial dialogue about the future of AI and its role in society. They have prompted researchers, policymakers, and the public to consider the ethical implications of AI and to develop guidelines and regulations to ensure that AI is used for the benefit of humanity. This ongoing dialogue is crucial for navigating the complex societal challenges and opportunities presented by AI.

The Unfinished Story: A Journey of Exploration and Discovery and the Current State of the Field

The story of artificial intelligence is far from over. It is a continuing journey of exploration and discovery, driven by human curiosity and the desire to understand and replicate the essence of intelligence.

The field continues to evolve rapidly, with ongoing research into new architectures, algorithms, and applications. The quest for AGI remains a long-term goal, and the potential for future breakthroughs is immense. Current research areas include:

- **Explainable AI (XAI):** Making AI decision-making more transparent and understandable.
- **Federated Learning:** Training AI models on decentralized data sources while preserving privacy.
- **AI for Science:** Using AI to accelerate scientific discovery in fields like biology, chemistry, and physics.
- **Neuromorphic Computing:** Developing hardware that mimics the structure and function of the human brain.
- **Robust AI:** Creating AI systems that are more resilient to adversarial attacks and unexpected inputs.

The field is also experiencing significant investment and activity, both from academia and industry. Major tech companies are investing heavily in AI research and development, and governments around the world are recognizing the strategic importance of AI. This level of activity suggests that AI will continue to be a major driver of technological innovation and societal change in the years to come.

As we move forward, it is crucial to remember that AI is not just a technology; it is a reflection of our own aspirations and a testament to our ingenuity. By approaching AI development with a sense of responsibility and a commitment to ethical principles, we can ensure that this powerful technology is used to create a better future for all.

Bibliography: Entirely accessed through Gemni & Claude

I. Foundational Texts and Historical Documents:

- **Turing, A. M. (1936). On Computable Numbers, with an Application to the Entscheidungsproblem.** *Proceedings of the London Mathematical Society*, 2(42), 230-265. (The foundational paper on the Turing Machine)

- **Turing, A. M. (1950). Computing Machinery and Intelligence.** *Mind*, 59(236), 433-460. (Introduces the Turing Test)

- **McCulloch, W. S., & Pitts, W. (1943). A logical calculus of the ideas immanent in nervous activity.** *The bulletin of mathematical biophysics*, 5(4), 115-133. (Early work on neural networks)

- **Shannon, C. E. (1948). A mathematical theory of communication.** *Bell system technical journal*, 27(3), 379-423. (Important for information theory, relevant to AI)

- **Minsky, M., & Papert, S. (1969). Perceptrons: An introduction to computational geometry.** MIT press. (Critique of early perceptrons)

- **Newell, A., & Simon, H. A. (1976). Computer science as empirical inquiry: symbols and search.** *Communications of the ACM*, 19(3), 113-126. (Important for symbolic AI)

II. Books on the History of AI:

- **Crevier, D. (1993). AI: The tumultuous history of the search for artificial intelligence.** BasicBooks. (A classic overview)

- **McCorduck, P. (2004). Machines who think: A personal inquiry into the history and prospects of artificial intelligence.** AK Peters/CRC Press. (Another influential historical account)

- **Nilsson, N. J. (2010). The quest for artificial intelligence: A history of ideas and achievements.** Cambridge University Press. (A more recent and comprehensive history)

- **Russell, S. J., & Norvig, P. (2021). Artificial intelligence: A modern approach.** Pearson Education Limited. (While a textbook, the introductory chapters provide valuable historical context)

III. Works on Specific AI Subfields:

- **Rumelhart, D. E., Hinton, G. E., & Williams, R. J. (1986). Learning representations by back-propagating errors.** *Nature*, 323(6088), 533-536. (Key paper on backpropagation)
- **Hochreiter, S., & Schmidhuber, J. (1997). Long short-term memory.** *Neural computation*, 9(8), 1735-1780. (Key paper on LSTMs)
- **Vaswani, A., Shazeer, N., Parmar, N., Uszkoreit, J., Jones, L., Gomez, A. N., ... & Polosukhin, I. (2017). Attention is all you need.** *Advances in neural information processing systems*, 30. (Key paper on Transformers)

IV. Articles and Reports:

- **Lighthill, J. (1973). Artificial intelligence: A general survey.** Science Research Council. (The influential Lighthill Report)
- Articles in *Artificial Intelligence*, *Machine Learning*, *IEEE Transactions on Pattern Analysis and Machine Intelligence*, and conference proceedings from AAAI (Association for the Advancement of Artificial Intelligence) and NeurIPS (Neural Information Processing Systems).

V. Online Resources:

- **AI Magazine:** Publications from the AAAI.
- **arXiv:** A preprint server for scientific papers, often containing cutting-edge AI research.

VI. Books on Related Topics:

- **Books on the history of computing:** These provide context for the hardware developments that enabled AI.

- **Books on cognitive science and neuroscience:** These offer insights into human intelligence and its relationship to AI.

- **Books on the ethical and societal implications of AI:** These are essential for addressing the broader impact of AI.

Glossary:

A

- **Algorithm:** A set of well-defined instructions for solving a problem or performing a task, often implemented by a computer.

- **Artificial General Intelligence (AGI):** Hypothetical AI with human-level general intelligence, capable of performing any intellectual task a human can. Also known as "strong AI."

- **Artificial Intelligence (AI):** The broad field concerned with creating machines capable of performing tasks that typically require human intelligence, such as learning, reasoning, and perception.

- **Artificial Neural Network (ANN):** A computational model inspired by the structure and function of the human brain, consisting of interconnected nodes (neurons) that process information.

- **Augmented Intelligence (IA):** Using AI to enhance human cognitive abilities rather than replacing them. Also known as "intelligence augmentation."

- **Automation:** The use of technology to perform tasks automatically, reducing or eliminating the need for human intervention.

B

- **Backpropagation:** An algorithm used to train artificial neural networks by calculating the error at the output layer and propagating it back through the network to adjust the connections (weights) between neurons.

- **Bayesian Network:** A probabilistic graphical model that represents the dependencies between variables, used for reasoning under uncertainty.

- **Big Data:** Extremely large and complex datasets that are difficult to process using traditional data processing methods.

C

- **Characteristica Universalis:** A universal language of reasoning envisioned by Gottfried Wilhelm Leibniz, based on symbolic notation.

- **Church-Turing Thesis:** The principle that any computable problem can be solved by a Turing Machine (and therefore by any general-purpose computer).

- **Cognitive Science:** The interdisciplinary study of the mind and intelligence, encompassing fields like psychology, neuroscience, linguistics, and computer science.

- **Common Sense Reasoning:** The ability to understand and reason about the everyday world in the same way that humans do.

- **Computation:** The process of performing calculations or logical operations, often by a computer.

- **Computational Power:** The ability of a computer to perform computations, often measured in terms of processing speed and memory capacity.

- **Connectionism:** An approach to AI that emphasizes the use of interconnected networks of simple processing units (neurons), as in artificial neural networks.

- **Convolutional Neural Network (CNN):** A specialized type of neural network designed for processing data with a grid-like topology, such as images.

D

- **Deep Learning:** A subfield of machine learning that uses artificial neural networks with multiple layers (deep networks) to learn complex patterns from data.

- **Difference Engine:** A mechanical calculating machine designed by Charles Babbage to automate the calculation of polynomial functions.

- **Distributed Computing:** Processing large datasets across a cluster of computers, allowing for faster and more efficient computation.

E

- **Expert System:** An AI program designed to mimic the decision-making abilities of human experts in a specific domain.

G

- **General Problem Solver (GPS):** An early AI program developed by Newell and Simon designed to solve a wide range of problems using heuristic search methods.

- **Graphical Processing Unit (GPU):** A specialized electronic circuit designed to accelerate the creation of images in a frame buffer intended for output to a display device. GPUs are also used for general-purpose computing, especially for training deep learning models.

H

- **Heuristic:** A problem-solving technique that uses practical methods or shortcuts to find a good solution, but not necessarily the optimal solution.

I

- **Image Recognition:** The ability of a computer to identify and classify objects or features within an image.

- **Internet of Things (IoT):** The network of interconnected physical devices, vehicles, appliances, and other objects embedded with electronics, software, sensors, and network connectivity, which enables these objects to collect and exchange data.

K

- **Knowledge Representation:** The way in which knowledge is encoded and stored in a computer system.

L

- **LISP:** A programming language developed by John McCarthy, widely used in early AI research, particularly for symbolic AI.
- **Logic Theorist:** An early AI program developed by Newell and Simon capable of proving mathematical theorems.
- **Long Short-Term Memory (LSTM):** A type of recurrent neural network designed to address the vanishing gradient problem, enabling the network to learn long-range dependencies in sequential data.

M

- **Machine Learning (ML):** A subfield of AI that focuses on developing algorithms that can learn from data without explicit programming.
- **Markov Decision Process (MDP):** A mathematical framework for modeling decision-making in situations where outcomes are partly random and partly under the control of a decision maker.

N

- **Natural Language Processing (NLP):** A field of AI concerned with enabling computers to understand, interpret, and generate human language.
- **Neural Network:** See Artificial Neural Network (ANN).
- **Neuro-inspired AI:** Approaches to AI that draw inspiration from the structure and function of the human brain.

P

- **Perceptron:** An early model of a neural network, consisting of a single layer of interconnected neurons.
- **Prolog:** A logic programming language often used in AI research, particularly for expert systems and natural language processing.

R

- **Recurrent Neural Network (RNN):** A type of neural network designed for processing sequential data, with feedback connections that allow it to maintain a "memory" of past inputs.

- **Reinforcement Learning (RL):** A type of machine learning where an agent learns to interact with an environment by taking actions and receiving rewards or penalties.

S

- **Semantic Analysis:** The process of understanding the meaning of words, phrases, and sentences in natural language.

- **Symbolic AI:** An approach to AI that focuses on representing knowledge using symbols and rules, and manipulating those symbols using logical reasoning.

T

- **Transformer Network:** A neural network architecture that uses attention mechanisms to weigh the importance of different parts of the input data, particularly effective for natural language processing.

- **Turing Machine:** A theoretical model of computation introduced by Alan Turing, consisting of a tape, a read/write head, and a set of rules.

- **Turing Test:** A test proposed by Alan Turing to assess a machine's ability to exhibit intelligent behavior equivalent to, or indistinguishable from, that of a human.

Endnote: Methodology & Purpose

Dear Reader,

Thank you for reading *Mind Machines: The Story of Artificial Intelligence*. You might be interested to know that this book was created entirely using generative AI large language models (LLMs). Specifically, I utilized Google's Gemini 2.0 Flash Experimental model and Anthropic's Claude 3.5 Haiku.

This project began one Monday evening while I was experimenting with Google's newly released Gemini 2.0 Flash, exploring the history of AI. I was struck by the detail and accuracy of its responses, particularly when the text was reviewed and refined by a second LLM. This prompted me to ask: "How feasible would it be to use these tools to write an entire book?" And so, I began.

My process unfolded as follows:

1. Gemini generated an initial table of contents.

2. I then asked Gemini to provide detailed notes for each chapter, emphasizing a cohesive narrative flow.

3. I initially attempted to have Gemini draft the entire book at once, but this proved impossible due to output size limitations.

4. I transferred the detailed outline to Claude and tasked it with writing the book. After drafting two chapters, Claude requested feedback, which I provided. It then completed a roughly 12-page draft.

5. This draft was then given to Gemini for critique, which resulted in a substantial amount of helpful feedback.

6. Following Gemini's suggestions, I had it rewrite each chapter individually.

7. After completing the rewrite, I again asked Gemini to review the revised chapters and provide further feedback, which Gemini then incorporated, chapter by chapter.

8. I compiled the entire book into a Word file.

9. I then asked Gemini to generate a table of contents for the Word document, which I subsequently added.

10. Gemini suggested ten potential book titles. I selected a few favorites and asked it to rank them based on their likely effectiveness on an Amazon listing. "Mind Machines: The Story of Artificial Intelligence" was ranked second.

11. I asked Gemini to describe three cover design concepts and then generate corresponding images. I selected my favorite design (with some minor adjustments in GIMP).

12. Finally, I asked Gemini for suggestions on other elements to include, resulting in the creation of the bibliography and glossary. Gemini also provided formatting recommendations.

In short, the entire process, from initial concept to final formatting, was heavily guided and executed by these powerful AI tools.

Five hours after beginning this experiment, I now hold a completed book that would have previously required a year or more of dedicated research and writing. I am deeply impressed by the potential of this emerging technology. I believe it will fundamentally change how we interact not only with computers but with information in general.

I encourage you, dear reader, to explore these technologies for yourself. The process is incredibly fun and engaging, and familiarity with these tools will likely become essential as more aspects of our personal and professional lives integrate with AI.

Thank you,

Sam

www.ingramcontent.com/pod-product-compliance
Lightning Source LLC
Chambersburg PA
CBHW071654240526
45469CB00023B/2427